Good news for everyone

Story by Penny Frank

Illustrated by John Haysom

THE LION
STORY BIBLE

49

TRING · BELLEVILLE · SYDNEY

The Bible tells us how God sent his Son Jesus to show us what God is like and how we can belong to God's kingdom.

This is the story of what happened to the disciples after Jesus had left them and gone back to be with God.

You can find the story in your own Bible, in the book of Acts, chapters 1 to 4.

Copyright © 1986 Lion Publishing

Published by
Lion Publishing plc
Icknield Way, Tring, Herts, England
ISBN 0 85648 774 0
Lion Publishing Corporation
10885 Textile Road, Belleville,
Michigan 48111, USA
ISBN 0 85648 774 0
Albatross Books
PO Box 320, Sutherland, NSW 2232, Australia
ISBN 0 86760 559 6

First edition 1986

Printed and bound in Hong Kong
by Mandarin Offset International (HK) Ltd

**British Library Cataloguing in
Publication Data**

Frank, Penny
  Good news for everyone. – (The Lion
  Story Bible; 49)
  1. Apostles – Juvenile literature
  I. Title   II. Haysom, John
  225.9′22   BS2440

  ISBN 0-85648-774-0

**Library of Congress Cataloging in
Publication Data**

Frank, Penny.
  Good news for everyone.
  Summary: After Jesus ascends into
  heaven, the apostles are visited by the
  Holy Ghost and go out to preach the
  word of Jesus and perform miracles.
  1. Apostles – Juvenile literature.
  2. Church history – Primitive and early
  church, ca. 30-600 – Juvenile literature.
  [1. Apostles. 2. Bible stories – N.T.]
  I. Haysom, John, ill.
  II. Title.
  BS2440.F69 1986   226′.609505
  85-13163
  ISBN 0-85648-774-0

Jesus had gone back to heaven to be with God. But his disciples had important work to do. They were to tell the whole world about Jesus!

'You will need God's special help,' Jesus said. 'So go back to Jerusalem and wait there.'

One day, when the disciples were all
together, praying, there was a sudden
noise, as if a gale of wind was rushing
through the house.

Then they saw what looked like
tongues of fire that reached out and
touched each one of them. They looked
at each other in amazement.

4

They began to speak, and found themselves talking in languages they did not even know. They felt very excited and full of joy.

'God has sent the special help that Jesus promised us,' they shouted. They made so much noise that a big crowd gathered.

The disciples forgot how frightened they had been. Now they wanted to tell the whole world about Jesus and God's kingdom.

Jerusalem was full of visitors from other countries, because it was the festival of Pentecost.

The disciples rushed outside and started to tell the crowd the wonderful story of Jesus.

Everyone could understand. Each of the visitors heard them speaking in his own language!

It was a miracle. God had given the
disciples the special help they needed to
tell the people about the kingdom of
God. They could not see Jesus any more,
but God had sent his Holy Spirit to live
in each of them, always.

7

The most amazing person to watch was
Simon Peter. When Jesus had died,
Simon Peter had been very frightened.
All he had wanted was to go back to
being a fisherman on Lake Galilee.

But now Simon Peter was filled with God's power. He stood up in front of everyone and explained the good news of God's kingdom. His face was shining with joy and gladness.

A few days later, Simon Peter and
another disciple, John, went to the
temple to worship God. They were full of
praise.

They wanted to thank God for the
special help he had given them.

As they went through the gate, they saw
a man who had never been able to walk,
sitting there asking for money.

Every day his friends brought him to
the gate, so that he could beg from the
people who were going to the temple.

'Please give me some money,' he called out to Simon Peter and John.

'We don't have any money,' said Simon Peter. 'But we do have something to give you. In the name of Jesus, I tell you to stand up and walk!'

Simon Peter took him by the hand, and the man stood up. His feet and legs became strong. He started to leap and jump about.

He went with them into the temple, shouting praises to God at the top of his voice.

When the people in the temple saw him,
they stopped what they were doing.

'Just a minute,' they said, 'aren't you
the man who sat at the temple gate?
What's happened to you?'

The man told them.

Simon Peter said, 'I don't know why you are so surprised. We didn't do this by ourselves. Jesus from Nazareth, whom you killed, was God's own Son. God raised him to life again. Now he has gone back to be with God, but God has given us his special power.

'Tell God you are sorry for what you did and he will forgive you. Believe us, Jesus is alive.'

Many people were excited to hear that Jesus was still alive, especially the people who had been healed by him, or had enjoyed listening to his teaching.

In the city of Jerusalem many people believed the good news of God's kingdom, and God gave them the special power he had given to Jesus.

Day after day, more and more people found that what the disciples were so joyful about was really true. Jesus was still alive!

The priests and leaders in Jerusalem were horrified to find that the disciples of Jesus were telling everyone that he was alive again.

'Stop telling the people about Jesus,' they told Simon Peter and John.

'We can't,' the disciples said. 'Jesus told us to tell the whole world.'

They told everyone they met about Jesus.

More and more people became followers
of Jesus. They often met together in the
temple, to thank God for his kingdom
and his help.

They often had meals together in each
others' homes. If anyone was poor, or
had no food, the others shared their food
or money with them.

They really loved each other. And they
knew it was because God was giving
them his special help.

He had made them into new people,
by giving them his own Holy Spirit.
They were completely changed.

The priests and leaders in Jerusalem
made up their minds to stop people
talking about God's kingdom. The
followers of Jesus were punished. They
had to leave the city and go to other
towns and villages.

But this was the best thing that could have happened.

It meant that the good news about God's kingdom was now being told to the whole world.

The Lion Story Bible is made up of 52 individual stories for young readers, building up an understanding of the Bible as one story — God's story — a story for all time and all people.

The New Testament section (numbers 31–52) covers the life and teaching of God's Son, Jesus. The stories are about the people he met, what he did and what he said. Almost all we know about the life of Jesus is recorded in the four Gospels — Matthew, Mark, Luke and John. The word gospel means 'good news'.

The last four stories in this section are about the first Christians, who started to tell others the 'good news', as Jesus had commanded them — a story which continues today all over the world.

Good news for everyone is from the first chapters of the New Testament book of Acts: the Pentecost story, from chapter 2; the healing of the crippled man, from chapter 3; troubles with the Jewish leaders, from chapter 4.

No one can see God's Holy Spirit. But Jesus had promised that when he went away he would send his Spirit to be with each of his followers for ever. He would show them the truth and help them to live as God wanted.

On the day of Pentecost, Jesus' disciples had no doubt that the Holy Spirit had come. Not only did they hear a sound like a great rushing wind, and see flames of fire that did not set light to anything. But they found that, instead of being frightened and hiding away, they were able to stand up in front of great crowds and tell them about Jesus — in their own languages. Nothing, no one, could stop them now.

The next book in the series, number 50: *Paul at Damascus*, tells the dramatic story of the great missionary apostle.